IT'S SCIENCE!

Time

IT'S SCIENCE!

Time

Sally Hewitt

W

FRANKLIN WATTS
LONDON•SYDNEY

First published in 1999 by Franklin Watts
This edition published in 2001

Franklin Watts
96 Leonard Street
London EC2A 4XD

Franklin Watts Australia
56 O'Riordan Street
Alexandria, Sydney
NSW 2015

Series editor: Rachel Cooke
Designer: Mo Choy
Picture research:Sue Mennell
Photography: Ray Moller unless otherwise acknowledged
Series consultant: Sally Nanknivell-Aston

ISBN 0 7496 4278 5

Dewey Decimal Classification Number 529

A CIP catalogue record for this book is available from the
British Library.

Printed in Malaysia

Acknowledgements:
Antique Clocks Gerard Campbell p. 13r; Eye Ubiquitous p. 15bl (Sean Aidan);
Frank Lane Picture Agency p. 25l (John Karmali); Image Bank p. 26tr;
Images Colour Library pp. 22, 23tl; Oxford Scientific Films pp. 20 (Richard Packwood),
23c (Owen Newman), 25tr (Martyn Colbeck); Planet Earth Pictures p. 23bl (Allan Parker);
The Stock Market p. 27c; Tony Stone Images pp. 23tr (Gary Vesta), 25br (Laurence Monneret),
27t (Alistair Beck). Thanks, too, to our models: Luke Jackson-Abeson, Nadine Gupta,
Thomas James and Fay Beaman.

Contents

What's the time?

Do you sometimes ask the question "What's the time?"

Do you know what time you go to school in the morning?

What time do you have lunch?

What is your bed time?

Do you go to school, have lunch and go to bed at the same time every day?

💡 THINK ABOUT IT!

What would happen if you went to school at any time you chose – not at the right time? Would your friends and teachers be there at the same time as you?

6

Knowing how to tell the time helps you to be "on time".

What happens when
you are early?

What happens when
you are on time?

What happens when
you are too late?

 TRY IT OUT!

Make a list like this one of some
of the things you will do tomorrow.

Can you write the time you should
be doing each one? Will it matter if
you are late for any of these things?

Wake up - 7 o'clock
Breakfast - 8 o'clock
School - 9 o'clock
Lunch - 12.30
Football - 4 o'clock
TV programme - 5.30
Supper - 6 o'clock
Bedtime - 8 o'clock

Time passing

You can't see time but it is always moving on. How much time passes while Adam makes his model?

It takes Adam an **hour** to finish the helicopter. Some of the things you do only take **minutes** or even **seconds**.

 TRY IT OUT!

Guess how long it takes you to brush your hair, clean your teeth or get dressed. Check your watch to see how long you actually take to do these things. Were you right?

Your hair is growing all the time but very slowly so you can't see it happening. It takes about 6 **weeks** for your hair to grow about 2 cm.

After you have been to the hairdresser's, how long do you wait before it is time to get your hair cut again?

A whole **year** passes between birthdays.

TRY IT OUT!

Have you got photographs of yourself on two birthdays in a row – perhaps your last birthday and the one before? Can you see how much you have changed and grown in the time it has taken for one year to pass? Can you still fit into clothes you wore a year ago?

9

Day and night

We see time moving on as day becomes night and night becomes day.

12 o'clock in the middle of the day is called midday or noon.

Daytime begins when the sun rises in the morning.

Afternoon is the part of the day that comes after noon.

Evening is at the end of the afternoon. The sun sets and it becomes dark.

THINK ABOUT IT!

What do you do at these different times of day?

12 o'clock in the middle of the night is called midnight.

Day and night happen because Earth, the planet we live on,
is a ball-shape spinning in space. It looks to us as though the sun is moving
across the sky, but really we are moving as Earth spins around.

It takes 24 hours, one whole **day**, for Earth to spin all the way
around once. The part of Earth facing the sun changes as it spins.

It is daytime when the
part of Earth you are on
is facing the sun.

It is night time when the
part you are on is facing
away from the sun.

 TRY IT OUT!

On a sunny day early in the morning, push a
stick into soft ground. Mark where the shadow
falls. Keep marking the shadow of the stick at
different times of the day. What do you notice?

Measuring time

Have you got a watch? Is there a clock on your kitchen wall? We use clocks and watches to measure time. In the past, people used candles, sand and water to measure time.

It takes an hour for the wax to burn down between the marks on this candle.

It takes 5 minutes for the sand to flow from the top to the bottom of this egg timer – just the time it takes to boil an egg.

 TRY IT OUT!

People used to measure time with a bowl that took a certain amount of time to sink. You can make a simple time measurer, too. Shape a shallow bowl from cooking foil. Use a pencil point to push a small hole in the bottom. Put it in water and time how long it takes to sink.

Watches and clocks have different ways of keeping time which are much more accurate.

A small **spring** inside this watch gradually uncurls to make the hands move around.

A **pendulum** swinging steadily backwards and forwards keeps some clocks in time.

Inside this watch is a battery with a piece of **quartz crystal** that is always moving back and forth a tiny amount. Each move back and forth always takes exactly the same time. Quartz watches keep very accurate time.

 LOOK AGAIN

Look again at page 7. Why do we need to measure passing time? Look again at page 11 to find another way to measure time.

Counting the hours

Clocks and watches measure time in hours, minutes and seconds. There are 60 minutes in an hour, and 60 seconds in a minute.

It takes about one second to clap your hands once.

It takes about one minute to build a tower this high.

It takes about an hour to bake a potato in an oven.

 LOOK AGAIN

Look again at page 11 to find out how many hours there are in a day.

The long hand on this clock face moves round to show the passing minutes.
The short hand moves much more slowly and shows the passing hours.

On a digital clock, the numbers on the left

of the 2 dots show the hours. The numbers on the right of the 2 dots show the minutes.

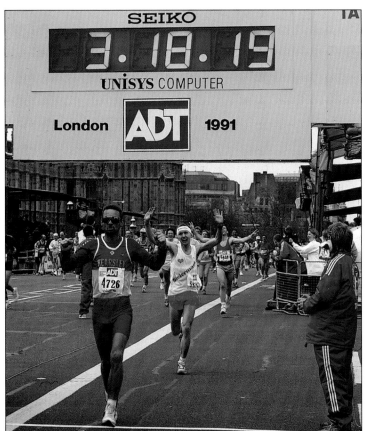

A stop watch can measure even smaller amounts of time than a second. Runners are often timed with a stop watch. Sometimes less than a second decides who is the winner of a race.

💡 THINK ABOUT IT!

What do you think you can do in an hour? What can you do that only takes a minute? What can you do in just one second?

15

What's the date?

A year is divided into **months**, weeks and days. You can check the date and find facts about a year in a **diary** or a **calendar** like this.

YEAR 2000

JANUARY

Sun	Mon	Tues	Wed	Thur	Fri	Sat
						1
2	3	4	5	6	7	8
9	10	11	12	13	14	15
16	17	18	19	20	21	22
23	24	25	26	27	28	29
30	31					

FEBRUARY

Sun	Mon	Tues	Wed	Thur	Fri	Sat
		1	2	3	4	5
6	7	8	9	10	11	12
13	14	15	16	17	18	19
20	21	22	23	24	25	26
27	28	29				

MARCH

Sun	Mon	Tues	Wed	Thur	Fri	Sat
			1	2	3	4
5	6	7	8	9	10	11
12	13	14	15	16	17	18
19	20	21	22	23	24	25
26	27	28	29	30	31	

APRIL

Sun	Mon	Tues	Wed	Thur	Fri	Sat
						1
2	3	4	5	6	7	8
9	10	11	12	13	14	15
16	17	18	19	20	21	22
23	24	25	26	27	28	29
30						

MAY

Sun	Mon	Tues	Wed	Thur	Fri	Sat
	1	2	3	4	5	6
7	8	9	10	11	12	13
14	15	16	17	18	19	20
21	22	23	24	25	26	27
28	29	30	31			

JUNE

Sun	Mon	Tues	Wed	Thur	Fri	Sat
				1	2	3
4	5	6	7	8	9	10
11	12	13	14	15	16	17
18	19	20	21	22	23	24
25	26	27	28	29	30	

JULY

Sun	Mon	Tues	Wed	Thur	Fri	Sat
						1
2	3	4	5	6	7	8
9	10	11	12	13	14	15
16	17	18	19	20	21	22
23	24	25	26	27	28	29
30	31					

AUGUST

Sun	Mon	Tues	Wed	Thur	Fri	Sat
		1	2	3	4	5
6	7	8	9	10	11	12
13	14	15	16	17	18	19
20	21	22	23	24	25	26
27	28	29	30	31		

SEPTEMBER

Sun	Mon	Tues	Wed	Thur	Fri	Sat
					1	2
3	4	5	6	7	8	9
10	11	12	13	14	15	16
17	18	19	20	21	22	23
24	25	26	27	28	29	30

OCTOBER

Sun	Mon	Tues	Wed	Thur	Fri	Sat
1	2	3	4	5	6	7
8	9	10	11	12	13	14
15	16	17	18	19	20	21
22	23	24	25	26	27	28
29	30	31				

NOVEMBER

Sun	Mon	Tues	Wed	Thur	Fri	Sat
			1	2	3	4
5	6	7	8	9	10	11
12	13	14	15	16	17	18
19	20	21	22	23	24	25
26	27	28	29	30		

DECEMBER

Sun	Mon	Tues	Wed	Thur	Fri	Sat
					1	2
3	4	5	6	7	8	9
10	11	12	13	14	15	16
17	18	19	20	21	22	23
24	25	26	27	28	29	30
31						

TRY IT OUT!

Use the calendar to check out these facts about a year.
How many months are there in a year?
There are 365 days in a year. Every four years there is a leap year – it has one extra day which makes 366 days. The extra day is in February, which is usually only 28 days long. Is 2000 a leap year?
Can you find your birthday on the calendar?
There are 7 days in a week. How many weeks are there in a year?

We often write the date like this: 8/7/00

This number shows the day.

This shows the month.

This number shows the year.

8/7/00

Can you find this date on the calendar?

A diary can help you to plan ahead and not forget important dates. It can help you to remember the things you have done, too.

A year

Earth does not just spin. It also moves in an enormous loop around the sun. It takes a whole year for Earth to go all the way around once.

Earth is tilted so that the half nearest to the sun is warmer while the other half is colder.

👁 LOOK AGAIN

Look again at page 11 to find out how long it takes for Earth to spin around once. Look again at page 16 to work out how many times it spins around in one year.

As Earth moves around the sun, the warmer half becomes colder, and the colder half becomes warmer.

This change from warm to cold and back again causes the **seasons**: spring, summer, autumn and winter.

THINK ABOUT IT!

What is the weather like at the moment? Do you think the part of Earth where you live is tilting towards the sun or away from it at the moment?

Seasons

The seasons change from spring, to summer, autumn, winter and then back to spring again. Each season brings different kinds of weather. Follow the arrows to see how the seasons follow each other during the year.

When spring comes, the weather starts to get warm after the cold winter.

Winter is the coldest season. Sometimes snow falls and you have to wear your warmest clothes outside.

In the autumn it starts to get colder again. Leaves on some trees begin to change colour and fall to the ground.

TRY IT OUT!

Make a seasons wheel.
You need 2 paper plates and a
paper fastener. With a pen, divide
each plate into quarters.

In the quarters of one plate,
draw a picture of each
season. Cut one quarter
out of the other plate,
leaving a section at its
centre to push the paper
fastener through.

Put this plate on top of the other
plate and fix them together at the
centre with a paper fastener.

Move the top plate round
to show each season
in turn.

Summer brings hot weather. It
is a good time to play outside.

21

Natural clocks

Plants and animals do not have clocks and watches like us.

They tell the time by sensing natural changes such as the weather getting colder or the days getting shorter.

These changes are rather like natural clocks that help them to know when to grow or when it is time to get ready for the cold winter ahead.

👁 LOOK AGAIN

Look again at page 10 to find something that happens naturally to wake you in the morning.

Spring is a good time for birds to lay eggs because the chicks will hatch in the summer when there is plenty of food around.

22

Flowers bloom in the warm summer sun. This is the time when there are plenty of insects around to visit them and carry **pollen** from flower to flower.

Flocks of swallows gather together at the end of summer. They know that soon there will not be enough to eat so they will make a very long journey to find food.

Autumn is the time that dormice fatten themselves up while there is still plenty of food.

They sleep all winter using up the food they have stored as fat in their bodies.

 LOOK AGAIN

Look again at page 20 to find what some trees do when the weather begins to get cold in the autumn.

Always changing

How long can you stand still for? Time never stands still, it is always moving on. Even if you stand still all day, things around you change.

People, animals and plants are always changing and growing.

 TRY IT OUT!

Plant some seeds in earth and put the pots in a warm sunny place. Water them and look out for the first signs of shoots. Watch how the plants change and grow a little bit every day.

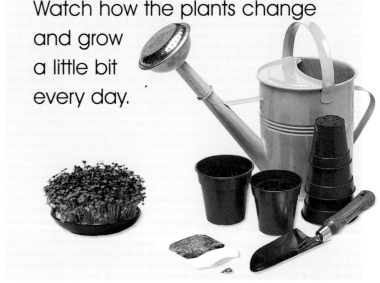

LOOK AGAIN

Look again at page 9 to find something that is always growing on your head.

Different creatures take different amounts of time to grow. Some are born tiny and helpless, others can look after themselves straight away.

This baby elephant will stay with its mother until it is 10 years old and it will not stop growing until it is about 25!

A baby bird can look after itself only a few weeks after hatching!

You will be fully grown when you are about 20 years old. But your body will still keep changing.

 THINK ABOUT IT!

Once you are a grown up, how do you think you will continue to change as you get older? What do you think you will look like when you are 20 years old? What do you think you will look like when you are 50?

25

Fast and slow

Everyone knows that a hare can run very quickly and that a tortoise lumbers slowly along. As long as the hare does not stop for a nap it will easily win a race against a tortoise!

The winner of a race is the one who gets to the finishing line first. They are the fastest – they have taken the smallest amount of time to run the race.

TRY IT OUT!

How fast can you write your name, put on your shoes and socks or deal a pack of cards in two equal piles? To find out, get a friend to time you using the second hand on a watch or clock, or use a stop watch if you have one. Try the tasks again. Can you do them faster?

THINK ABOUT IT!

Is it always a good idea to do something very fast? Can you think of anything that you should do slowly?

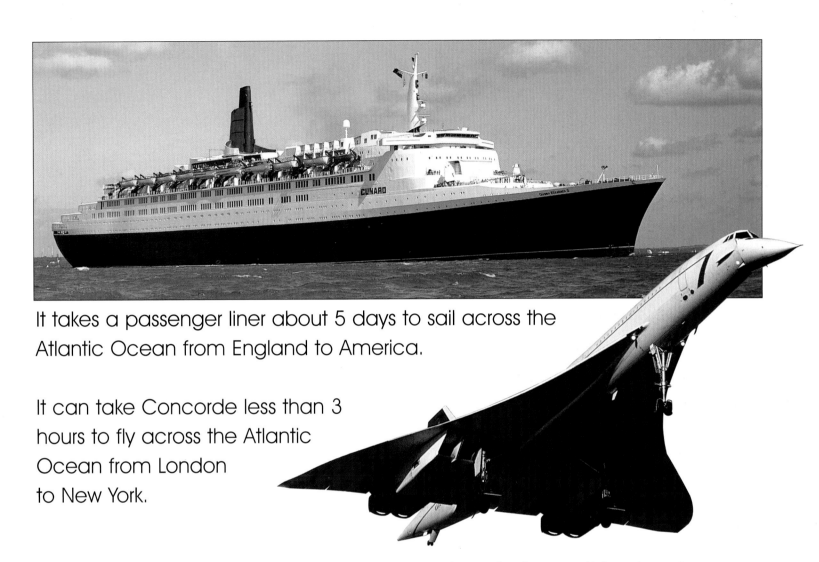

It takes a passenger liner about 5 days to sail across the Atlantic Ocean from England to America.

It can take Concorde less than 3 hours to fly across the Atlantic Ocean from London to New York.

We often need to measure how fast something is going – its **speed**. A **speedometer** measures the speed of a car in kilometres or miles per hour. If a car's speed is 50 kilometres per hour (31 miles per hour), it will travel 50 kilometres (31 miles) in one hour.

Signs on the roads tell traffic how fast it is allowed to go. Drivers have to check their speedometers to make sure they aren't going too fast.

Useful words

Calendar A calendar lists the months, weeks and days of a year. It shows on which day of the week a particular date falls.

Day A day is the time it takes for Earth to spin around once. It is 24 hours long. Sometimes, we use the word "day" to describe the time when it is light, between sunrise and sunset.

Diary A diary is a book that is divided into days, weeks and months. You write dates to remember or things that have happened in it.

Hour A day is divided into 24 hours. It takes 1 hour for the big hand on a clock to go all the way around. There are 60 minutes in an hour.

Minute An hour is divided into 60 minutes. If you count to 60, saying your name between each number, about a minute will have passed. There are 60 seconds in a minute.

Month A year is divided into 12 months. Most months are 31 days long, except April, June, September and November which have 30 days, and February, which usually has 28. In a leap year, February is 29 days long.

Pendulum A pendulum is a hanging weight which swings backwards and forwards at a constant speed. Some clocks use pendulums to keep time.

Pollen Pollen is the yellow dust in flowers that plants use to make seeds. Pollen has to be moved from one flower to another to form a seed.

Quartz crystal Quartz crystal is a type of rock. A tiny piece of crystal is used inside the batteries of some watches and clocks to keep time.

Season On certain parts of Earth, the seasons change through a year from spring to summer, autumn and winter. Each season has different weather which affects plants and animals.

Second A second is a small amount of time, about the length of a hand clap. There are 60 seconds in a minute.

Speed Speed is how fast something is going. Fast and slow are words we use to describe speed. We measure speed by seeing how long it takes something to move a certain distance.

Speedometer A speedometer is an instrument for measuring speed.

Spring A spring is a piece of wire that has been coiled round and round. If it is squashed or stretched it will try to push or pull itself back into shape. "Spring" is also the name we give to the season after winter, when the weather starts to become warmer.

Week There are 7 days in a week: Monday, Tuesday, Wednesday, Thursday, Friday, Saturday and Sunday. We call Saturday and Sunday the weekend.

Year A year is how long it takes for Earth to move all the way around the sun. There are 12 months and 365 days in a year. Every fourth year is a leap year when there are 366 days.

Index

About this book

Children are natural scientists. They learn by touching and feeling, noticing, asking questions and trying things out for themselves. The books in the It's Science! series are designed for the way children learn. Familiar objects are used as starting points for further learning. Time starts by asking what's the time and explores the different ways we measure time and see time passing.

Each double page spread introduces a new topic, such as natural clocks. Information is given, questions asked and activities suggested that encourage children to make discoveries and develop new ideas for themselves.
Look out for these panels throughout the book:

TRY IT OUT! indicates a simple activity, using safe materials, that proves or explores a point.
THINK ABOUT IT! indicates a question inspired by the information on the page but which points the reader to areas not covered by the book.
LOOK AGAIN introduces a cross-referencing activity which links themes and facts through the book.

Encourage children not to take the familiar world for granted. Point things out, ask questions and enjoy making scientific discoveries together.